THE MACHINE INSIDE ME

The Machine Inside Me Professional Endorsements

ENDORSEMENT #1

Michelle Steffes' book **The Machine Inside Me** is one of the most effective books I've read on the power of reframing thoughts and rewiring the mind. Remarkably, **The Machine Inside Me** can be effectively used with both adults and children because of its simple and practical presentation. I recommend it for counselors, therapists, educators, parents, grandparents, employers, ministry workers, health providers and anyone else who wants to learn how to guide our children to learning how to heal their brain by reframing negative thoughts and transforming their thinking.

Shelly Beach, M.A. (Education)
ITR-CTSC(ITR-Certified Trauma Support Coach)
Teacher of the Year (Awarded by Walmart)
Multiple Award-Winning Author, Speaker, Consultant
Co-Founder of PTSDPerspectives.net and PTSDPerspectives on Facebook
For more info: Helpfortrauma.com

ENDORSEMENT #2

"I had the privilege of reading this GAME-CHANGING book for children. Wow! **The Machine Inside of Me** teaches children about the amazing and powerful things their brains can do and how. It teaches children to navigate their own emotional triggers and employ self-leadership skills. This is what makes a strong, confident adult. Based on settled brain science, I have SEEN first-hand this information change lives. Education/ Information are the key and THIS book is a great place to start."

Wanda Sanchez, PTSD/Trauma Support Coach, Co-Author of the 2015 Selah Award Winning, 2015 Golden Scroll Non-Fiction Gold Merit Award, and the 2015 Readers Favorite Gold Medal Winner

ENDORSEMENT #3

"**The Machine Inside of Me** gives children and adolescents enmeshed in negative self-talk an understanding of how such thoughts impact the wiring of their brains. The author, Michelle Steffes, uses kid-friendly imagery and vocabulary to make sense of the role hormones can play in either perpetuating or reducing negative thought cycles. Best of all, she leads readers through simple yet powerful exercises and activities to help them make new habits that lead to improved mental health. If you love children who are struggling with unresolved trauma, depression, or anxiety, get them this book."

Jolene Philo, National Speaker, 30 yr educator and author of "Does My Child Have PTSD? What To Do When Your Child Is Hurting from the Inside Out"

THE MACHINE INSIDE ME

How to change your brain and discover the power within you!

Michelle L. Steffes

The Machine Inside Me

Published in the United States of America by Credo House Publishers,
a division of Credo Communications LLC, Grand Rapids, Michigan
credohousepublishers.com

ISBN 978-1-62586-237-2

Cover and interior design by Rob Rice
Editing by Donna Huisjen
Illustrations by Rob Rice

Printed in the United States of America
First Edition

CONTENTS

START HERE

The Machine Inside You

What if you were not completely human, but a machine? What if you had buttons and switches that would allow you to turn off or tone down emotions such as anger or hurt and turn up love or compassion?

What if you had some kind of electrical box that would dial up more energy or dial down for better sleep at times when you needed it?

Or you possessed the ability to draw people to yourself or intentionally repel them away from you through thought alone?

When it comes to learning, wouldn't it be amazing if you could wire in the knowledge you needed to score high on a test or excel in a new skill?

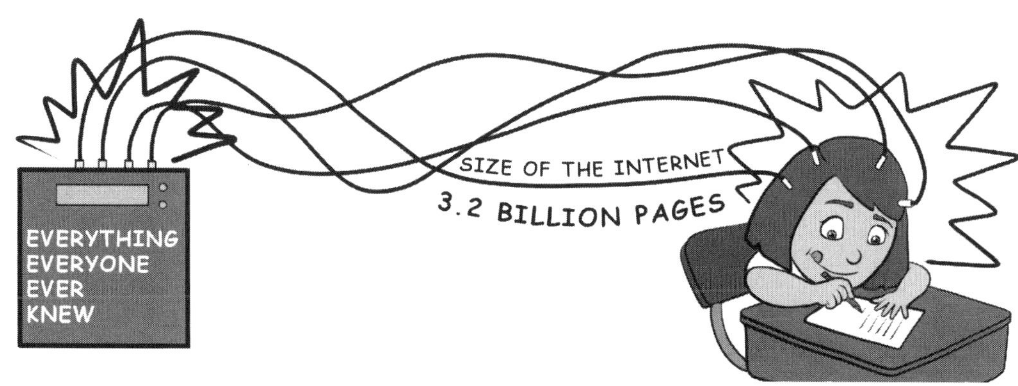

The journey you are about to take will reveal secrets you may never have known about yourself. You'll learn that you have superpowers built into your brain, heart, and body. These powers act much like a machine, and when we learn how to navigate the buttons and switches, they can give us incredible power.

Our story begins with two young people a lot like you! As you read this book, pay close attention to the struggles they faced and how they resolved these struggles by learning how to operate the "machine" inside them.

Chapter One

Liam's Story—The Inner Battle

Liam and Anna were both adopted and lived in a small home just outside a tiny town in Nebraska.

Liam, who was nine years old, loved to pretend he was a race car driver and had a dog named Max.

His older sister, Anna, was almost thirteen years old, and she liked to dress up and pretend she was a glamorous movie star. Every time she did, Liam would just roll his eyes.

Most of the time they got along, but they did not play together as much as they used to when they were younger.

Liam often struggled in school because he could not seem to focus or sit still in the classroom to learn.

Whenever a teacher called on him to give an answer, he felt embarrassed and ashamed.

He wanted to do well, but it seemed as though there was a force inside of him that would not allow him to pay close attention for more than three minutes at a time.

Whenever Liam failed an assignment or test, he hated himself more and more, feeling as though the teachers hated him, too. This made him sad and frustrated.

And to make matters worse, his parents were not happy with him when he came home with a failing grade. He knew they loved him, but it did not feel that way sometimes.

It seemed as though the entire world was against him—except for Max, his dog, who truly became his best friend.

As time passed, Liam grew angry inside—angry at himself and at everyone who saw him as a failure. The anger and embarrassment he felt made his lack of ability to focus even worse and created in him more of the same emotions.

Whenever he would try to explain what was happening or how he felt, he was told things like "Stop making excuses" or "You can do it—just set your mind to it!" Despite the good intentions of those who said these things, they felt like write-offs and made him think about his failures even more.

Whenever he was frustrated, some of his friends would shy away and seem disinterested in playing with him.

Liam would lie awake at night sometimes, rehearsing the thoughts of the day over and over in his head. He didn't know whether he should cry or scream because of the feelings that welled up with each thought. These were the nights he could not get to sleep. Max would often creep up extra close to him to cuddle, as though he could sense that something was wrong.

Liam did not know it, but inside his brain he was installing lots of bad wiring.

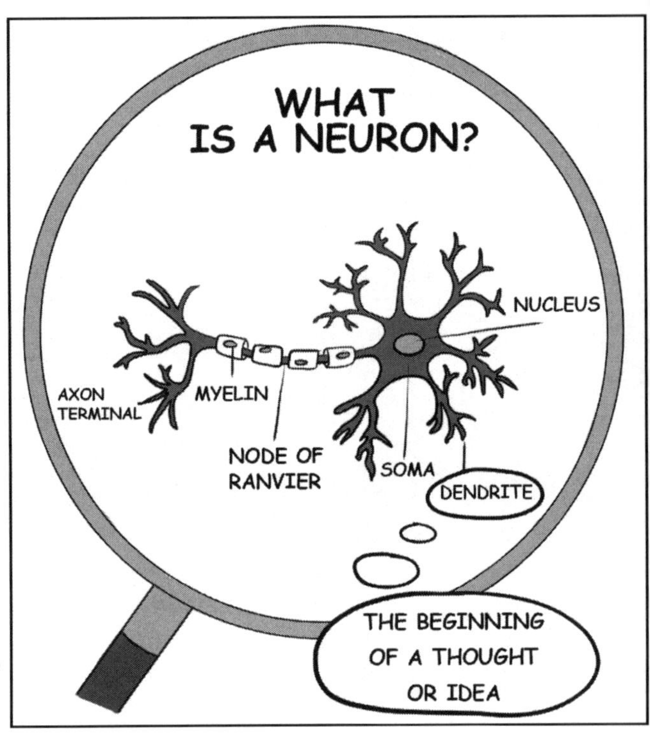

His brain had been created with one hundred billion neurons from the time he was born. Their purpose was to equip him with the power to store his ever-expanding knowledge of new skills, new concepts, and new data so he could use it later.

Since the brain is like a machine, it was up to Liam to program it. His brain itself did not determine whether the programming was good or bad, whether it would give Liam superpowers to win in life, or whether it would create bad wiring that would make him struggle.

With every new thought, his neurons were creating electricity at four hundred billion actions per second. This electricity was using the protein from his body to form new wiring, connecting the neurons together like the wiring inside a radio or car. This process happens amazingly fast in each of us, forming patterns in the brain called neural networks.

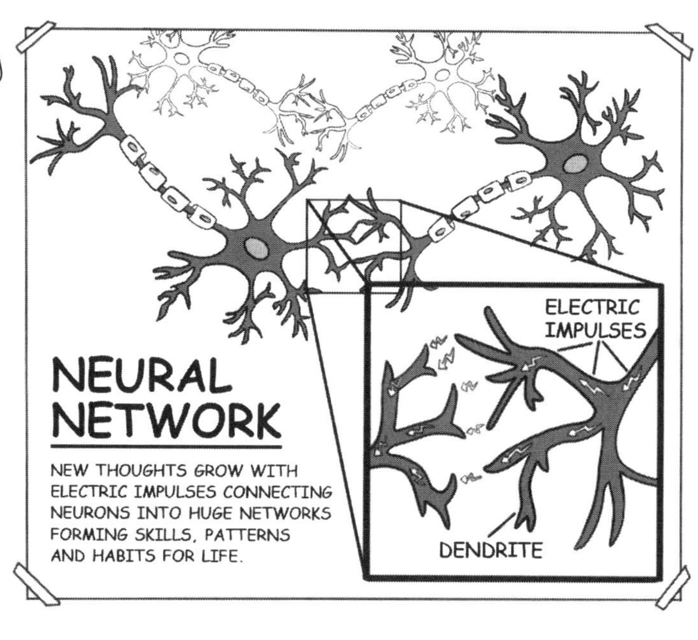

Every time Liam felt down on himself, angry, or frustrated and spent time thinking about it, he was either adding more wires to his machine or strengthening the neural networks he had already created, making them even more powerful and full of electricity.

The stronger and more electrified the wires became, the harder it was for Liam to stop thinking about everything that was wrong in his life.

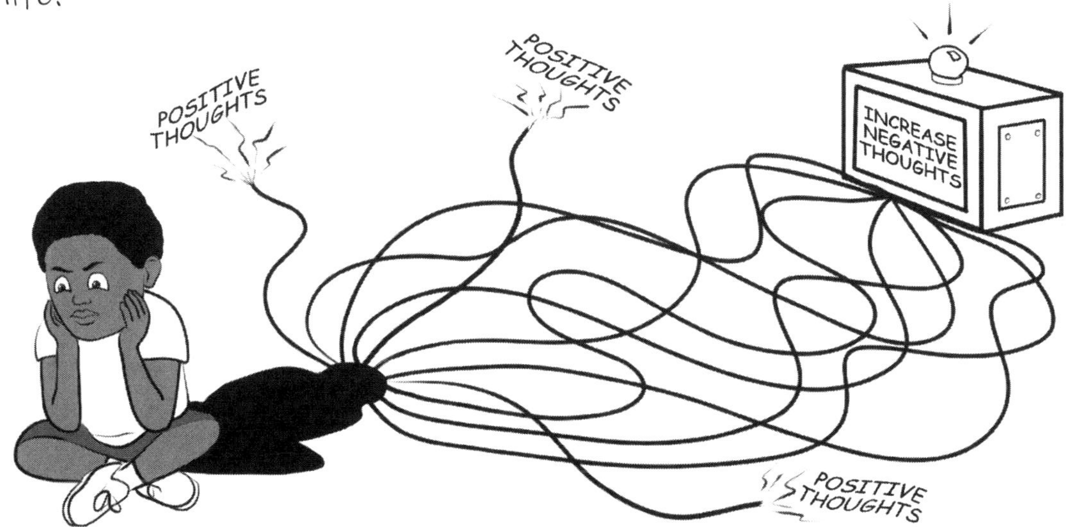

TUNE UP THE MACHINE – WIN THE INNER BATTLE:

In the spaces provided below, write out three things in your life right now that make you feel hurt, angry or upset. In a later chapter, we will show you how you can use your superpowers to rewire your machine, win the battle inside and change how these events affect you.

Inner Battle #1 - ____

____

____

____

Inner Battle #2 - ____

____

____

____

Inner Battle #3 - ____

____

____

____

Chapter Two

Anna's Story—Trying to Fit In

Anna knew Liam had struggled in school and tried to help whenever she could. However, she had many of her own growing pains.

As a twelve-year-old going on thirteen, she found the idea of her little brother tagging along a bit awkward.

In fact, she was changing so much that this frustration was creating a gap between her and Liam. This made her sad because she had always loved her brother, but she was also excited about the many new things going on in her life.

Unlike Liam, Anna was a great student, and she was quite popular. Her girlfriends would often come over to do each other's hair and paint fingernails.

Liam thought she had the perfect life. However, he did not know that Anna felt self-conscious about her looks.

Anna had not yet experienced the signs of adolescence many of her girlfriends had.

Even though some of them were a little older, she thought she was ugly and was privately worried about whether her body and appearance would catch up with theirs.

Despite her frequent selfies on social media in different poses and with different expressions and the pretty clothes she wore, she just did not feel adequate inside.

Anna's parents and many of her friends would tell her how pretty she was, but she did not believe it.

She did not talk to anyone about this because she was scared about sharing her personal struggles and did not want to draw attention to herself.

She wanted people to think she had it all together, even though she did not. Her constant habit of comparing herself to others, especially on social media, was beginning to affect Anna's health.

She would often tell herself that she was fine and just overreacting. But on some days, her doubts overwhelmed her to the point that she got headaches and asked to stay home from school. Sometimes she was given permission and other times, she was not.

On the days she had to attend school, she would put on a good act.

Anna would smile and act as though everything was great, hoping no one would notice the battle going on inside.

The day came and it was Anna's 13th birthday. After a short celebration, Anna went with three of her friends to the local skate park to check out the action and see if they could meet some of their other friends there.

Out of the corner of her eye, she noticed three local boys coming across the yard right towards them.

She was so nervous and tried to hide how she felt. At first, she thought that they wanted to wish her a Happy Birthday and she was a little excited!

However, her hopes were quickly dashed to the ground when the boys paid more attention to her older friends and never even mentioned her birthday.

She just laughed and joined in the conversation but felt uncomfortable, especially when they started ignoring her entirely.

That night, Anna's parents could tell something was wrong, but she would not talk about it. She said very little and went up to her room earlier than usual.

Anna began rehearsing the events of the day repeatedly in her head, questioning what she may have said or done wrong.

Only hours before, she was happily enjoying a fun birthday celebration and now all she could remember was the encounter with the boys and her friends.

She felt so alone and so rejected. She curled up into a ball in her bed and cried quietly that night until she finally fell asleep.

Weeks, even months went by with more encounters occurring that were like the park incident. Just like Liam, Anna was creating negative neural networks in her brain that would affect her even more in future encounters.

As Anna continued to reject herself and experience dissatisfaction with her own appearance, she became increasingly sullen and withdrawn in her days at home.

Despite her ability to put on a good show for her friends at school, she was convincing herself inside that she was ugly and would go home each night completely drained of energy and hurting.

As a result of her inner thoughts and the turmoil she was creating, the relationship with her parents began to deteriorate. Each time Anna's parents would try to console her or speak to her, she would snap at them or just walk away.

Even Liam could not seem to get near her anymore. The tension in the house was steadily increasing with each passing month.

TUNE UP THE MACHINE – WIN THE INNER BATTLE:

In the spaces below, write out three examples of ways in which you may be hurting those around you by how you are responding to your feelings. In the next chapter, we will help you to sort through the pain you may be feeling from those relationships, rewire your machine, and discover new strategies to win.

Example A - ______________________________

____

____

____

Example B - ______________________________

____

____

____

Example C - ______________________________

____

____

____

Chapter Three

Changing the Fluids—Altering Brain Chemistry

Just as machines need oil, gas, and other fluids to run properly, the brain creates neurochemicals (***nur·ow·keh·muh·kls***), also called neurotransmitters.

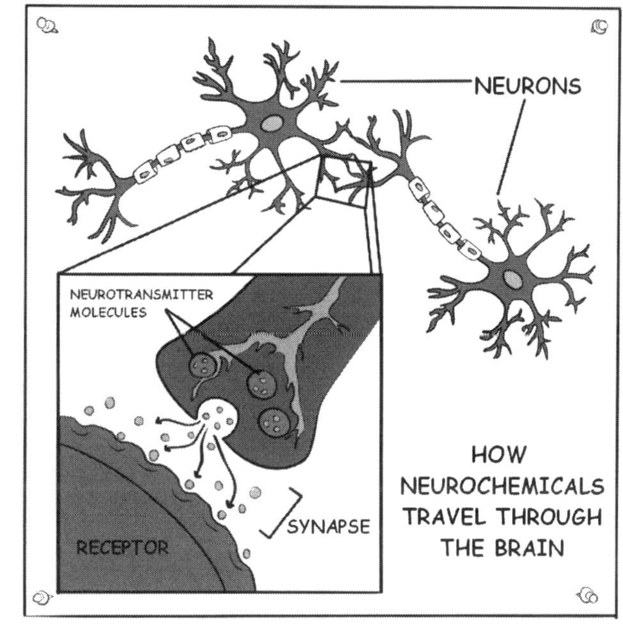

When you think thoughts, whether good or bad, a reaction occurs within each connection of neural pathways. This connection is called a synapse (***si·naps***). Between these synapses are many tiny, tube-like openings called receptors.

They receive the chemicals or fluids being released from each of your neural pathways during the process of thinking. Understanding how this works will give you the superpower to choose which fluids you will allow to be released.

About sixty neurochemicals are surging through your brain and body. Some of these create a feeling of happiness. Examples are dopamine (***doh-puh-meen***), serotonin (***se-rah-toh-nin***), oxytocin (***ok-se-toh-suh-n***), and GABA. But we will just give them fun names, like Dopie, Sara, Oxy, and Gabby.

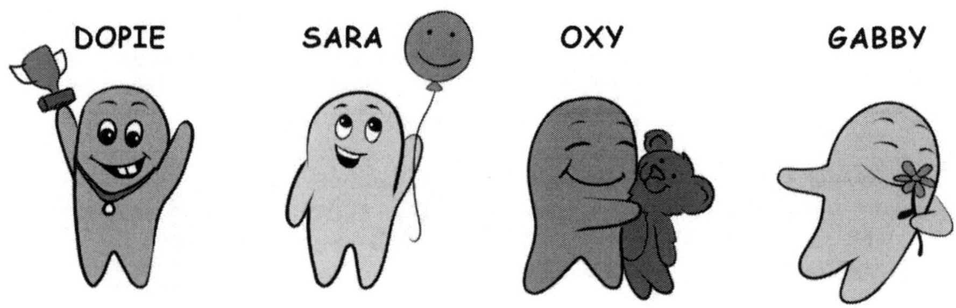

Other, stress-related chemicals released in the brain can make us feel sad, hurt, frustrated, or angry. These are called names like cortisol, (***kor-ti-zul***) adrenaline, (***uh-dr-eh-nuh-len***) or norepinephrine (***nor-ep-i-neffren***). We will call them Cort, Adren, and Norpin.

The machines inside Liam and Anna created and strengthened many new and painful neural networks as the brother and sister thought about the frustrations, disappointments, and painful moments of their lives. But these machines were also altering the neurochemicals in their brains and throughout their bodies. You can see from these examples that, when we choose to let anger or resentment build up in our hearts and minds over time, we begin to feel more and more angry or offended.

Below is a brief explanation of seven of these neurochemicals.

Remember that, with each thought and emotion, these neurochemicals move through the receptor sites in our brain, creating strong feelings that drive our responses to life's challenges. When you learn to hit the right switches and change the fluids that are running through your machine, you can win every day!

- Cort (cortisol). Short visits from Cort are okay, but too many too often will affect our ability to sleep, focus, concentrate, and manage our emotions effectively. This can lead to frequent illness, tummy aches, and even some food allergies.

- Adren (adrenaline). Adren can help us because it is designed to give us super strength when we are in danger. Too much for too long, though, can result in anxiety, depression, and even weight gain.

- Norpin (norepinephrine). Norpin shows up when we are angry, upset, or afraid. This can affect our ability to think clearly, make us sweat, cause headaches, and make it harder for us to fight illness. Norpin can also make us restless and hyperactive.

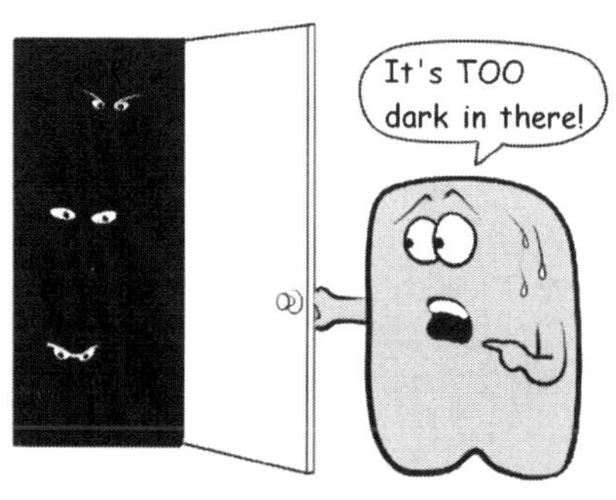

- Dopie (dopamine). Dopie is referred to as the "reward neurochemical." Every time we do well on a project, win a game, or make someone proud of us, Dopie is there, making us feel happy and amazing!

- Oxy (oxytocin). Oxy comes along when we feel loved, appreciated, or accepted. Oxy is responsible for building strong relationships and giving us that warm feeling when we have a crush on someone.

- Sara (serotonin). Sara is always hanging around when we feel good about ourselves and are happy. Sara is also there to help us sleep well and stay healthy.

- Gabby (GABA). Gabby is there to help us stay calm. Increased amounts of this neurochemical keep us from feeling too scared, nervous, or frustrated. Gabby appears when we reframe our thoughts using our superpowers. Gabby makes Cort and Adren run away and stop bothering us.

TUNE UP THE MACHINE – WIN THE INNER BATTLE:

Now that you have a clearer understanding of the characters behind your moods and emotions, try to identify the neurochemicals involved in the battles and examples you listed in Chapters 1 and 2 (place an X in each box where it applies).

Mark the column of each character that may be involved in the battles you listed in Chapter 1.

BATTLE	CORT	ADREN	NORPIN	DOPIE	OXY	SARA	GABBY
1							
2							
3							

Now see if you can identify the characters involved in the examples you wrote about in Chapter 2.

BATTLE	CORT	ADREN	NORPIN	DOPIE	OXY	SARA	GABBY
1							
2							
3							

Chapter Four

Realizing Your Superpowers—Reframing and Rewiring

OUR SUPERPOWERS

The good news is that we can turn on the switch to our superpowers by choosing to change our thoughts. But how do we do this when the feelings are strong—especially when we have allowed ourselves to expand the wiring of our machines to the point that it seems impossible to stop them?

Below are some powerful superpowers we can use to shift gears and turn off the flow of these toxic fluids that make us sad, hurt, frustrated, or angry:

SUPERPOWER 1 - Change the Fluids (neurochemicals)

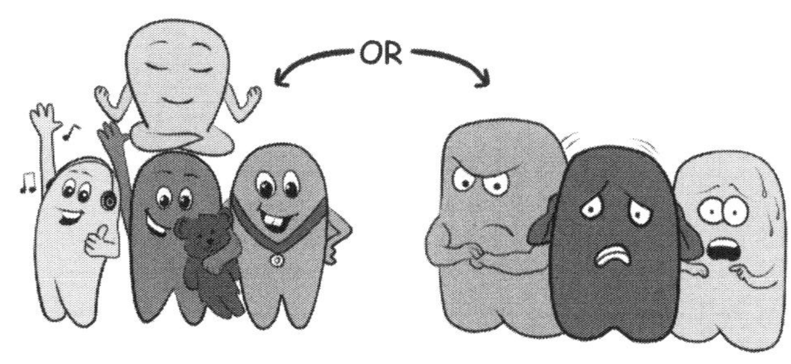

We can "change the fluids" (the neurochemicals) in our machine that control what we are feeling at any given moment.

In the beginning of this book, the question was asked, "What if you had buttons and switches that would allow you to turn off or tone down emotions such as anger or hurt and turn up love or compassion?"

Let's tackle a few of Liam's challenges considering this question and the knowledge we've gained so far.

Liam imagined the whole world was against him because of his struggles in school and the anger he felt inside. Each time he thought about his failures and allowed stinking thinking to consume him, he was creating more and more bad wiring (negative neural networks).

This was only programming his brain to produce more and more bad thoughts. It invited Cort, Adren, and Norpin to come in and invade his brain, making him feel even worse.

LIAM'S MIND HAS BEEN A PLAYGROUND FOR NORPIN, ADREN, AND CORT WHICH MAKES LIAM'S MOOD TERRIBLE.

One day, Liam read a book like this one and learned that he could "change the fluids" in his machine. He decided to rewire himself by choosing new ways of thinking.

He started by creating new habits to help him choose better ways of thinking. Liam began listening to messages that made him feel strong and happy.

He read books that helped him make better decisions. He got up every day thinking words of kindness about himself and of thankfulness for the blessings in his life, even on the days he did not feel like it.

Within a few weeks, Liam started to feel different about his abilities.

When he did not understand something, he was brave enough to ask for help. When he started feeling bad, he learned to reframe his thoughts by thinking about what he was good at instead of what he struggled with.

In a few months, he noticed that the pushy thoughts created by the bad wiring were slowly being replaced by good thoughts from the new wiring.

Just like a machine that had its engine tuned up and new fluids put in, Liam's brain began to slowly push away Cort, Adren, and Norpin replacing them with Dopie, Sara, Oxy, and Gabby. This made Liam excited about learning more.

Each time Liam stuck to his new habits and used his superpowers, he grew inside, feeling stronger and more focused. He also became more aware of those times when Cort, Adren, or Norpin were trying to come back and make him feel bad again.

LIAM HAS LEARNED HOW TO CONTROL HIS THINKING AND HAS CHOSEN POSITIVE THOUGHTS.

Because he stayed with his new habits, he got faster at shifting his thoughts, making him feel more powerful to succeed in his schoolwork and even helping him sleep better at night. We will discuss many of Liam's new habits in the next chapter, so keep reading! The best is yet to come!

SUPERPOWER 2 - Reframe & Shift Gears

When we learn to shift our machine into a new gear by changing the way we see something, this is called "reframing."

It is impossible to have thoughts of anger and thoughts of gratitude or compassion at the same time. We can choose to allow the good thoughts and turn away the toxic thoughts. Here are a few examples:

Someone at school takes part of your lunch without asking or tries to cheat from your paper. These are things you would naturally feel angry or frustrated about. In that moment, you can stay in that mode of operation and release the toxic fluids that only make you angrier. Or you can shift gears in your mind and think something else, like:

"Maybe that person doesn't have money for food at home and is too scared or ashamed to ask for help."

"Maybe that person can't read well, doesn't understand the work, has no one to help them with homework, or is afraid to ask a question."

"Maybe that person is unhappy with their life and is reacting to the toxicity in their body and brain. I'm thankful I have people who can help me. Maybe I can be the one to help them."

This is another form of the reframing mentioned earlier. It can help you resist the temptation to think the worst and end up releasing more Cort, Adren, and Norpin.

SUPERPOWER 3 - Program in New Habits & Patterns

As you learn to adopt new habits that give you the power to control what is happening inside you, this third superpower is automatic.

Anna had a problem of comparing herself to other girls she thought were prettier or better than herself. She kept a lot of hurt inside since she was not willing to talk these feelings through with anyone else. This was causing Cort, Adren, and Norpin to build up to a point that they were affecting her health, her sleep, and her energy levels.

She had worked so hard on this kind of wiring that she could no longer see good in her life. All the bad wiring in Anna's machine had programmed her to see only the things that made her feel sad, lonely, or hurt.

In fact, much of what Anna struggled with came from her own imagination. The imagination is powerful, and our machines will produce the wiring we create, whether or not what we imagine is real. In many ways, Anna became her own worst enemy, with Cort, Adren, and Norpin visiting her day and night.

One day, Anna's teacher asked if she could stay during lunch and talk for a few minutes. She had noticed Anna's struggle and offered to be her friend. Anna was reluctant, but the teacher shared that she had experienced some of the same struggles when she was younger. She gave Anna a special notebook and encouraged her to write down the good things she saw in her life every day.

In a couple of weeks, Anna realized how negative she had been about herself and her life. She began seeing herself differently. Anna's teacher continued to share new habits, which Anna agreed to try. For the first time, Anna was willing to open up to someone and take steps that would heal her heart.

After about a month, she discovered a whole new person emerging from inside her. Anna's parents and many of her friends also noticed the changes. Life began to evolve into something beautiful instead of the dark, lonely tunnel she had been creating.

As Anna continued with these new habits, she learned to appreciate her own beauty and stopped comparing herself to others. Her headaches went away, and she started reaching out to others, encouraging them in the same way her teacher did with her.

Anna became attractive to others because of her love and compassion. Even Liam felt that he had gotten his big sister back, and they enjoyed spending time together.

Anna's world was opening all around her! Life was suddenly good, and she was no longer afraid to share with others. Even the boys who had ignored her before began to pay attention to her.

Soon we will discuss the habits Anna's teacher taught her so you can experience the same transformation Anna did. It all begins with you!

SUPERPOWER 4 - Shift Your Energy to Attract

Both Liam and Anna had programmed themselves to think about their bad qualities and their concern about not fitting in. This had created negative energy they did not talk much about.

Remember how Liam's dog seemed to know something was wrong with him and snuggled close to him at night? Have you ever noticed that animals can sense when you are fearful? Have you ever been in a room with people you knew did not like you or were mad at you? You had a certain "sense" about it. How about when you walk into a room where people are arguing? Can you feel the tension?

This "sense" we have is real. When we are upset, nervous, or angry, others notice it. This is important to understand if we want to change how we come across to others. The best way to change this is to apply what we have talked about in this book, along with the habits we will discuss in the next chapter.

Just like Liam and Anna, you can learn to master reframing, rewiring, and changing the neurochemicals in your mind and body. The more you practice good habits and activate your superpowers, the more you will begin to see the magic of transformation.

But it all begins with you. No one else can change how you feel about yourself or your future. No one else can rewire your machine for you.

TUNE UP THE MACHINE – WIN THE INNER BATTLE:

Now that you understand four of your most effective superpowers, write below which superpower will help you deal with the areas you listed at the ends of Chapters 1 and 2. Then think about how you will begin this new journey of transformation.

Think about the three inner battles from Chapter 1 and the three examples from Chapter 2. Put a ✓ by the best superpower(s) you can use like tools to help you release the characters (neurochemicals) and rewire your machine.

BATTLES (CH. 1)	SUPERPOWER 1 Change the Fluids (neuro-chemicals)	SUPERPOWER 2 Reframe and Shift Gears	SUPERPOWER 3 Program in New Habits and Patterns	SUPERPOWER 4 Shift Your Energy to Attract
1				
2				
3				

EXAMPLES (CH. 2)	SUPERPOWER 1 Change the Fluids (neuro-chemicals)	SUPERPOWER 2 Reframe and Shift Gears	SUPERPOWER 3 Program in New Habits and Patterns	SUPERPOWER 4 Shift Your Energy to Attract
1				
2				
3				

Chapter Five

Daily Habits that Transform—A Blueprint to Win

In this chapter, we will begin exploring new habits you can create. If you apply them every day, you can rewire your machine, tune it up, and win more inner battles than ever before. How you apply the habits and how long you stick to it will determine the difference in how you think, feel, and function.

IMPORTANT INFORMATION ABOUT REPROGRAMMING WITH NEW HABITS:

If you do not continue to practice on new changes and act on them, your new wiring will dry up and go away in only two days! This is because your brain (machine) will keep only what it thinks you absolutely need.

If you do not use the new wiring, the brain causes it to "denature"—to fall off so your machine can make room for more new wires. This is your brain's way of being efficient and running clean.

That is why, when you learn new things like math or languages, you need to practice using your knowledge over a period of time. As the saying goes, "Use it or lose it."

New ways of doing things cannot become habits unless you stick to them every day for at least three to four weeks. This empowers your machine to develop full-size wiring networks that make practicing these new habits easier as time goes on.

If you quit these habits even after three or four weeks, your machine will slowly lose the new wiring you created. So, it is important to stay committed for the long term. If you use your superpowers to stick with powerful habits, you will notice changes by the third week. If you do not give up, your thinking and functioning will only get better from there on!

New Daily Habits that Transform

NEW HABIT 1—Feed the Machine

Like Liam, choose to read or listen daily to powerful and encouraging messages, found in books, audiobooks, podcasts, and videos. This habit will force your machine to grow new wiring, giving you incredible ideas and strength to defeat the inner battles of every day. The more you do, the more you will notice changes happening inside—changes that will invite Dopie, Sara, Oxy, and Gabby to hang out, chasing away Norpin, Adren, and Cort.

NEW HABIT 2—Use Your Internal Superpowers

You will believe what you say to yourself more than what others say about you. Therefore, when you hear bad things said about you, if you repeat them over and over in your head, you create wiring in your machine that will cause you to malfunction. Choosing to use your superpowers to reframe and rewire daily will dramatically alter how you think and respond.

NEW HABIT 3—Intentional Daydreaming

No matter how old you are, dreaming and imagining are part of your life. Many of us spend a lot of time imagining what could go wrong. Try to be more aware of what you are thinking about. You can even be intentional about what you imagine—try to imagine what you want to happen. Even if your dreams don't follow the same pattern as your imagining, you will still carry around more of Dopie, Sara, Oxy, and Gabby because of your decision to wire in better thinking patterns. Remember, the more Liam and Anna thought about the bad things, the sadder, sicker, and more defeated they felt, and the more they invited in Norpin, Adren, and Cort.

NEW HABIT 4—Light Up the Brain

Did you know that what you write out by hand stays in your memory much longer than what you type or text? This is because to write out something by hand you must light up both the left and the right hemispheres of your brain. The left side is more about logical thinking, and the right side is more creative. Handwriting requires both.

As Anna learned from her teacher, writing is a proven therapy method for those who are hurting. She began the habit of writing about the good things in her life. But even writing out your hurts can help you to release them more quickly and effectively—as long as this is not the only thing you write about. This is why so many people journal or keep a diary. Another benefit: when you handwrite action plans, you are much more likely to follow through. Even one or two sentences each day can make a huge difference.

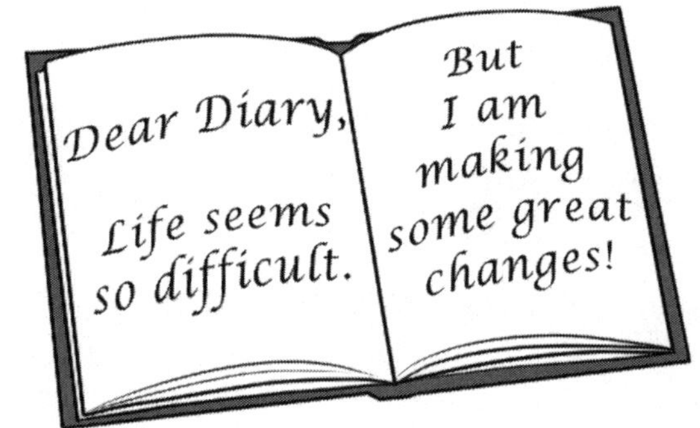

NEW HABIT 5—Create a Blueprint

For any building project to go successfully, there has to be a written plan or blueprint. This blueprint must be thought out in advance and must consider all obstacles and details if the builder is to succeed. Life can be the same way. If you do not write down specific goals you want to work on, tasks you need to accomplish to get there, and the methods of rewiring each will take, nothing will improve. Just like Anna and Liam, you must take deliberate action by creating a clear and powerful blueprint you can follow. Start with just five goals and break them down into three to five tasks you can do each day that will create the wiring required to meet those goals. Then start over with five new goals and repeat.

NEW HABIT 6—Optimum Machine Maintenance

All machines require maintenance. That includes electric toys, computers, and even robots. Your machine is no different; if it is neglected for too long, the maintenance issues will get worse and require a lot more to fix. The following are three major maintenance items to keep your machine running well:

#1 EXERCISE: First, let me introduce you to another kind of neurochemical. The neurochemicals in this category are called endorphins (*en-dor-fins*). Their function is to give you energy, reduce pain, and help release more Dopie and Sara so you can feel great. You release endorphins through lots of physical activity. Sitting still for too long can have the opposite effect. Exercise also sends more oxygen to your brain, helping you think better and feel more awake. Once endorphins are released during thirty to sixty minutes of exercise, the effects can last up to two full days!

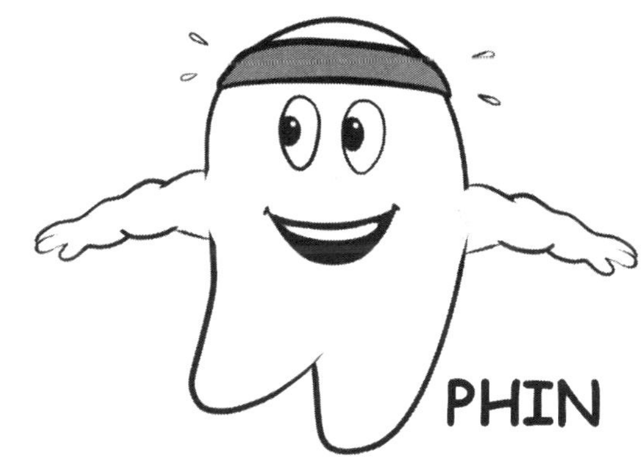

#2 OXYGEN is maintained through deep-breathing exercises that increase the presence of Dopie and Sara, while chasing away Adren and Cort, the stress-related neurochemicals. Any time you

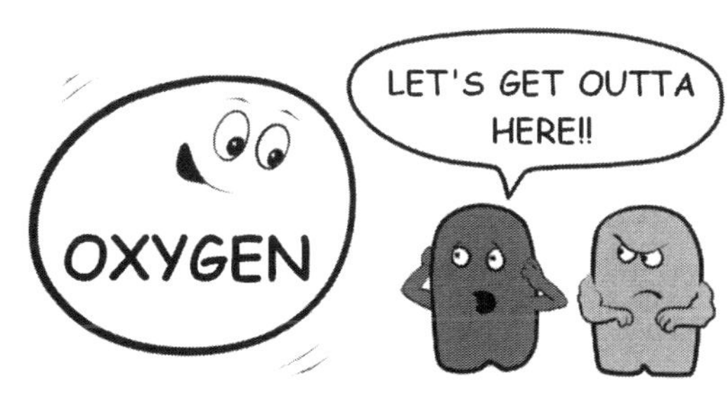

feel tired or anxious, try "box breathing": breathe in deeply for four seconds, hold your breath for four seconds, breathe out completely for four seconds, and repeat for two or three minutes. You should notice a difference in how you feel.

#3 WATER is key to machine health as well. Your machine is made up of two-thirds water. Hydrating yourself is as important as making sure a robot gets enough oil so it can run smoothly. Without enough water, you will feel tired, experience headaches, struggle with learning, and even feel sad or grouchy. Remember that you cannot substitute sugary drinks for water. Too much sugar slows down your machine.

NEW HABIT 7—Stay Thankful

The fastest and most powerful way to consistently release Dopie, Sara, Oxy, and Gabby is choosing to think about what is good in your life; about what you are thankful for. Thankfulness can be found in simple things, like a warm bed, clothes, the beauty of nature, and the people who care for you. Make it a goal to write out eight to ten things you are grateful for every day. This act alone is a huge game changer for removing bad

wiring and replacing it with good wiring. It enables a constant flow of happy, strong, and powerful neurochemicals. Write these things on your bathroom mirror, journal them daily, or write them on cards to post in your locker at school. The more you practice gratitude, the stronger you will become to fight off stinking thinking.

NEW HABIT 8—Giving Back

Another fast and powerful way to release Dopie, Sara, Oxy, and Gabby is doing good to others. Make this a daily goal, and watch the difference it makes. Anna discovered this once she gained enough confidence to encourage others. You can do things like holding the door open, saying thank-you more often, helping someone in need, or encouraging someone who is feeling sad or alone. A kind smile and thoughtful compliment can change the world around you and increase the flow of positive neurochemicals in you!

TUNE UP THE MACHINE – WIN THE INNER BATTLE:

Write down the new habits you want to apply and create a plan of action—a blueprint to build a new life. Only then will you see real changes magically happen inside of you and around you. You have the power within you! This is all about the daily choices you make! You are a machine designed to win!

Using the chart on the next page, fill in the first line of each box with five new goals you want to work on over the next thirty days. A few examples might be: wiring in more knowledge to improve my grades - saying nicer things to myself - feeding my mind better things - helping others in need - reframing bad thoughts.

In the next row, choose at least five new habits you will need to adopt to make these goals part of your daily routine. (Choose from the habit suggestions in this chapter or make up your own based on what you have learned)

Use the third row to write in daily tasks you will need to perform to achieve your blueprint.

BUILDING A TOP PERFORMANCE MACHINE—MY BLUEPRINT

5 GOALS TO ACCOMPLISH OVER 30 DAYS
(changes you want to see in your life)

1	
2	
3	
4	
5	

5 NEW HABITS I WILL WORK ON DAILY
(use suggested habits in Chapter 5)

1	
2	
3	
4	
5	

MY DAILY TASKS:
REQUIRED TO ACCOMPLISH ALL GOALS AND HABITS

MONDAY	TUESDAY	WEDNESDAY	THURSDAY	FRIDAY	SATURDAY	SUNDAY

FINAL THOUGHTS

Congratulations! The journey you just took revealed secrets you may never have known about yourself.

You learned that you have superpowers built into your brain, heart, and body. Now that you know how to work the buttons and switches inside you, what will you do with them?

Life is challenging, and things will happen that hurt, anger, or offend you—that is just a fact. However, no one but YOU can or will create change in you.

The choice is always yours.
"The Power is Within You!"

ABOUT THE AUTHOR

Michelle L Steffes author of "Reframe and Rewire: Greatness Through Daily Routine" provides real solutions from the painful experiences of her youth and over 10,000 hours of study in human behavior.

As a speaker, corporate trainer and executive coach, leading teams for over 25 years, Michelle has learned that the most important requirement for success is not what happens around us, but what happens INSIDE of us. When we can learn to reframe our perceptions, rewire how we think, act, and react, we equip ourselves with the ability to rise above every situation despite challenges.

In today's incredibly challenging world, Michelle grew an intense passion to help the leaders of tomorrow by authoring a book specific to ages 9-14. The intention is to empower them to discover their greatest potential through a daily shift away from self-defeating mind sets and habits.

www.ipvconsulting.com

ABOUT THE ILLUSTRATOR

Rob Rice has been an illustrator and animator since graduating from the Art Institute in Chicago, Illinois, in 2008. He loves to bring stories to life that build character and inspire readers to feel good about themselves and accomplish great feats.

In 2017, Rob had his greatest challenge yet. He lost his dominant right hand in an accident. He then taught himself how to draw and paint with his left hand and was able to continue to do what he loves.

www.robriceillustrations.com